TREMORS

Vibrations

Enough To Rearrange The World

Northfield Women Poets

HEYWOOD PRESS
NORTHFIELD, MINNESOTA

Grateful acknowledgment to *Sidewalks* for an earlier version of "Mourning;" *Rag Mag* for "Bone Lion" and "My Mother's Body;" *1995 Regional Writers' Competition Anthology* for "Photo of a Woman With Long Hair."

Heywood Press
5048 Ebel Way
Northfield, Minnesota 55057
Books may be ordered from the above addr

Cover art, "Padua," 10 1/2 x 8 1/4 oil on paper
© 1987 by Jil Evans
From the private collection of Karen and David Wee

<u>Editors</u>
Susan Thurston Hamerski
Beverly Voldseth
Karen Herseth Wee

ISBN 1-882699-04-1

Foreword

The Northfield Women Poets consists of ten or so prickly women who vacillate between ecstasy and suicide, find solace in the everyday and concrete, and occasionally are seized and fly, which makes everything worth it.

Several members have personal histories that read like florid prose, and all of their interior landscapes teem with life, to say the least. Like all women, they are common women, elemental—lifegivers, sustainers, furies—intimidating as hell, simple and gentle as the paper-skinned grandmother you think you know.

Enter into their poetry. We guarantee you'll see your own face in some of it. And you might be drawn to write your own, which is the whole point.

> —Trina Zelle,
> *member 1983–1989. Presbyterian*
> *minister, El Paso,Texas currently*
> *involved in a women's economic*
> *self-development project on the*
> *U.S./Mexican border.*

CONTENTS

TREMORS

Vibrations

Enough To Rearrange The World

MARY MOORE
EASTER

LIFE'S A SOUP

Cold soup's nice in summer
made from still-life vegetables
to soothe a sun-hot body.
But a cold stove's no way to cook
a soup to stay November.
Hot soup requires a fire
and movement, changes,
transformation wherein
sticking is a possibility,
a burnt mess at the bottom of the pan.

You have to lift the lid to stir the pot.

Some say hidden desires are best.
Keep the lid on they counsel,
turn down the fire.
Blessed are the restrained.
But there's no way around it.
You simply cannot force
the spoon through the closed pot top
eyes shut
wrist agitating the unseen.
No, no.

You have to lift the lid to stir the pot
and face familiar contents at a rolling boil.
Nothing new for dinner.

IF I SAID

If I said whatever I wanted to say
it would come out in one long howl
that the world doesn't want to give me
what I want when I want it,
a long screeching howl from deep in the throat
moving up to echo in the back of my head
and all the cavities of my skull.

If I said what I want
it wouldn't be responsible and accepting
not patient and mature
but urgent and full of insistence.
Hear my howl right now
know its meaning in the part of you
that would howl, too
if it could say whatever it wanted.

The howling voice says
don't keep turning away
stop hiding
come out from behind your wall
skip over the beginning
and start right in the middle
of hot emotion, protest, anger
need, hurt, disappointment.
The howling voice sets off tremors
vibrations enough to rearrange the world
capture all awareness
put its own priorities first
snap the population to attention.
Surround me surround me confront me
know me and let me know you back.

MY DARK BODY

for dark women everywhere

Eye of obsidian set in pearl
ivory bones
chambered ruby pumps blood
through sapphire veins
lungs like silken parachutes
arches, hollows, curves
of Byzantium.
My webbed fibers form
the labyrinths of souks
and tented bazaars.
Fruit flesh spills seeds
and ripeness
in the marketplace of many rhythms.
My dark body, unplundered treasure
encased in rare mahogony.

CONTACT IMPROVISATION

If only the world could know
the benediction of pure touch
the uncomplicated blessing
of skin to skin to ground
and flesh to bone in motion,

these whirling bodies
twisting in air
could send their magic spirits
into all our cramped conceptions,
lay to waste the narrow equation
of touch equals sex
equals sin equals stop
before you feel.

We could live the pleasure
of our feet touching the earth
in each step, weight sinking
through layers of time
meeting the sinking touch
of all the world
in the earth's molten core.

DANCER AT FIFTY-THREE

Sometimes, now, I can't quite imagine it
that rage to move
which used to satisfy and multiply itself
in any open space.

Early denied in me, cast aside for
pleasures more concrete,
its bud burst late into a room
with bars at all the lighted windows,
and sprung me out to flower.
It pressed me hard, once released,
doubled my desire for
all of me in the curving moment,
all of me in the air.

Motion, that unwilled spark
of heart, breath and blood
that separates us from rocks
yet binds our atoms with the same laws,
motion flows in and out of all of us.

But sometimes, for seconds, now,
the ghost of that raging dancer
enters this body and I fly again
breathing twenty-year-old breath
singing through loose joints
in love with the world.

COMING BACK

I detour and delay
seek out sweet words and sliding touch
to stave off reentry,
want to hover in the moments
before house becomes home,
before this bruised heart
becomes cell and solitary destiny.

At the threshhold
I scale a mountain of mail
junk and treasure indistinguishable,
find dead phones
and the lurking presence of bats.

I close doors against this greeting
from the bed I have made
and must inevitably lie in,
settle into the arms of the guest room
white-walled, bare
holding only my childhood bed
which takes me back
without judgment
until tomorrow.

IN MY MOTHER'S EMPTY HOUSE

It had nothing to do with envy.
My greed for her clothes
was a greed for her
a way to wear her
on my body
scent and body oils
spirit and laughter
draped on me
in a dark blue suit.
I filled my suitcase
in secret
in her empty house
in secret
with no one to watch.
Only her empty bed
to witness me
keeping her alive
in an armful of dresses.

MOMENTS BEFORE

She sits in the square chair
no longer straining on the hospital's pot
to expel death from her body.
The labored breath of three nights calms.
Bitten fingernails tip the piano hands
that rest in her lap.
Mama sits, turning her cheekbone to seek
pale sun through the blinds.
She warms visibly as light
and shadow stripe her face.
My breath calms,
my skin warms with hers.
Margaret, the nurse and I hover
around her, a suspended trio
unknowing in these moments before.

       I think this calm can last forever
       through all change of place and position.
       We will rest not just in the square chair
       not only in the sun by the window
       or the hospital bed
       but rest all the way into my far house
       its living room transformed for her living,
       its vivid space welcoming the years of her past.

Our trio, Margaret, the nurse and I,
bends low, a dance to lift her up.
Her raised hand stops us
"a little while longer"
is all she says.
Surveying worlds and time
she warms the upright minutes,
looks at her feet, stretches out her legs
brownfreckledwhite
like all the women in our family.
Stretches as if she planned

to stand and walk
away from the stroke
away from the mystery of her night flights
away from the unexplained miracle
of her morning returns
to this bed of monitored waiting.

       Calm sun in February kept death in hiding.
       This evened breath
       these stretched legs
       sent him, swinging cloak
       and glittering blade,
       into a seam of life's fabric
       stitched tight for one more hour.

When she agrees to go to bed,
to leave the chair, the sun,
only she knows what readiness
she is announcing.
In three-quarter time our trio
recommences the dance
of lifting her up,
of shift of weight from seat to standing
a quarter turn and swivelled hip
from chair to bed
supported by our bodies.
How could so gentle a minuet
rip death from his hiding place,
free this dark hooded escort
to claim his traveller?

       No, not like that
       no graceful dance
       but awkwardness of limbs
       and feet that were never
       in the right place
       a movement puzzle
       we could not solve
       as we jerked and twisted

pulled and lifted
and finally dropped her
backward onto the bed
her eyes jolted wide with a presence
we could not comprehend.

My back was turned when he strode in,
an entrance alive in the mirror of her face.
I twisted to find his head
in the tall rack of the nurse's gurney,
his feet among the silent rolling wheels
his body the bed that would take her.

Agitation returned to her breath,
everything cycles in this room,
coming round and round again.
That grunted effort at the end of each inhale
refilling her body with strength
in the acceleration of its rhythm,
fearful preparation for the drama
of her crossing.

She confronts him head on
"Say the twenty-third psalm!"
she commands us, fighting fire with fire,
combatting darkness with pure light.
We are her armies.
We speak "I shall not want!"
she urges us on
"He preparest a table!"
she is travelling quickly
"Thy rod and thy staff they comfort me!"
in the confusion of battle
rattled tongues, flailing hands
minds addled by mystery.
"Yea, though I walk through the valley
of the shadow of death!"
Are we guarding her or sending her?

"I will fear no evil!"
Only she knows what readiness
she is announcing.
"I will dwell in the house of the Lord
forever!"

Mama, come back, I shout
as her gaze fixes in her future.
For one moment
she travels back to me
to my face,
one look that says
        if it could be done
        I would do it for you.
The last collision of love
and eternity.

ANDREA EEN

IN THE SELKIRKS, 1973

I. Abbott Ridge

> All afternoon
> maddened by the stream
> I wait at the campsite
> footsore
> searching for your shape
> on the green mountain.
>
> When you return
> it is gone from your finger
> all of $15 from Goldfines
> consecrated in ritual
> witnessed by more
> than we bargained for.
>
> Foolish dreams
> half-drowned
> by whitewater.

II. Balu Pass

> Porcupine battle over
> we sleep in the mountain hut
> tethered by steel
> to frail grass
> mummies on a wood bench.
>
> Next morning there are
> gnawed marks on shingles
> and picnic table
> breakfast of cheese, raisins
> hard bread, grainy coffee.
> We stumble down
> a meadowed mountainside
> blue gentian, columbine

white daisies.
Wet fern fronds
lick our faces
rarefied
dizzy with love.

ANNIVERSARY

Sunday in July
     miles apart, an ocean between
     I remember
     buzzing summer sounds
     purple flowers trailing from a clothesline
     gleam of silver and dull stoneware in
     tissue paper cocoons
     interlaced murmurs of conversation.

We form an uneasy alliance
     playing the couple in ritual celebration.

Midday we falter
     seeking each other
     a refuge in music, our true marriage.

Strange, bright day
     focus of hopes
     I remember
     miles apart, an ocean between.

BLACK ICE

Crystalline, jagged cracks

      memory of uneven cooling

          and expansion.

I skate across fractures

         in thin sunlight

gliding from you

        back to you

smiling

    smiling.

MORNINGS

I am dead to all feeling
tight smiles conceal
snake-slithering despair
lucent fat insulates the knotted
rope which I cannot push through
to ream this grief.
A serpent
bunched in shadowed
night-blooming branches
coils in convolutions of muscles
tiny nerve fibers
constricts
no breath
I die a small death
today.

TABOO DEFORMATION FOR ST. VALENTINE'S DAY

I am your Hunter:
> you my honey-eater
> brown one
> moon-howler berserker.

I am your Gatherer:
> you are *honig*
> yellow waxy combed
> nutmegged glaze.

I face the sun:
> from my sinister side
> comes snow-laden wind
> carrying your musk
> south.

Oh, come to me,
> *My Sweet William*
> *My Sweet Pea, My*
> *Sweet Bittersweet.*

NIGHT MARRIAGE

Illinois 1973

Tomatoes fecund
fruit pendulous
corn leaves embrace the fat husk.
Moonlight deflects through glass louvers,
you inside me
as we rock the Great Lakes trailer.

Florida 1977

Night jasmine blooms outside this
flamingo pink house,
podocarpus filters the moon.
In lavender-blue April
jacaranda flowers rain down
slowly. You worried asleep.
I stare into tropical night
smelling spicy citrus, crushed
rotting.

Minnesota 1992

Our bed is broken; we nestle
low to the floor high up in the
trees. The corner streetlight
invades. I cry. You turn away
in your dream. Scent of burnt
old maids wafts from the puffed
rice factory, like kernels left long ago
in Grandma's blue Harlequin bowl.

CELESTIAL BODIES

We two bodies
being of sane minds
orbited different planets.

I chose Venus:
        you sabotaged my desires.

You chose Mars:
        I sabotaged your red
        clouded anger.

These skills we honed long ago
in our separate galaxies.

All we ever knew
        beyond the sublime music
        we played together:

So much empty space
        a few stars between.

SHOSTAKOVICH AT THE QUARTERBACK CLUB

You are there again, three-quarters turned away
smoking, coffee cup on the plastic table
sitting alone in the fishbowl window
unmistakable square head
mouth turned deeply downward
so many years of exile
losing friends to snowy wastes
prison, suicide.

Master of the Heroic
Master of the Banal

You look out at the ducks waddling
from the river, rise from your chair
with the remains of a hamburger lunch. I watch you
carefully crumble the bread on the grass, straighten
look up. I mouth the question through the glass.

You answer, a faint loosening of the downward curve
and walk with the ducks toward the Cannon River
your Neva.

I stare at that familiar river
of eagles, skunks, beaver.
Don't just survive, you said
endure.

POEM TO AN UNKNOWN LOVER

I see through your eyes
to sky twilit with dusk
seagulls flying out of your hair
toward a sliver of moon.

What is this shiver about
you whom I do not know?

Your limbs are graceful as
a gazelle on the Serengeti
but you are here in the polar latitudes
and I am sliding southward off the map.

Your heart is tweedy
matted like old pipe tobacco
prickly with caution
a raised nap.

This time find me a small place
an obscure chamber in your soul.

This time save me
from all of you.

OJO DE DIOSA

In the desert
it is sometimes wise
to live underground.
Beaks, fangs, thorns
surround.
Cholla jumps,
scorpion's tails lash
our brilliant colors.

The creosote bush releases
its acrid odor. Black branches are
spider lines of kohl, pungent
after warm rain.

Strangely beautiful
to live with danger.
Floods a sudden hazard—
earth not able to absorb
such abundance. Rain runs
through every crevice and
gully as tears ravage age lines.

The Goddess says:

> *Cry these tears.*
> *Keep danger at bay.*

MARIE VOGL GERY

A LOVE POEM NOT TOO SOON

Two killdeer rise quick from winter grass
flash white undershinings
caught between longing and pleasure
we lie in bed and whisper against old silence
above us invisible wind-owls mourn
death carried on their wind
the radio alarm announces
poison inhaled easily as the purple
of iris and lilacs still to bloom
star wars plans for bulbs of death
shot and planted across continents
no need to hear more, you snap off this news
turn to me, the phone rings

At your desk you take off your wedding ring
roll it like a child's hoop
learn again it is not perfectly round
those flat spots of wear
this ring cast only for us melds loss
with love and the hope for a future
tulips deep purple each spring
our oneness imperfect slowly blooming
season after season round about
closer than roots and earth
important as wing and wind

Another April will the killdeer rise
the wind-owls mourn before dawn
will all the dead be stars
the world no longer round nor flat
caught inside some black hole will our children
love and whisper into the silence
until their voices sing on the wind
in tongues they are yet to learn
peace, l'chaim, alleluia, amen

I-90: JANUARY

Wind sculpts this snow
long and slender
in hollows next to the road

Sunmelt and cold winds
create one after one after one
bodies of winter women

Asleep on their sides
arms above their heads
knees slightly bent

My eyes follow ankle, calf
thigh, hip, waist, breast
woman curved into woman

Each one asleep now
too cold to dream
lies under the cold sun

Fragile prey of elements
sun, wind, rain,
and man

Curved one into the other
they steal my dreams
from the stars

Dressed with skeletons
of summer's wild grass
tatooed by tracks of snowbirds

Late afternoon sun
pushes purple shadows
paints woman seals

In this deep winter sea
pinnipeds—selkies
wait to swim into spring

Today, the only warmth
steam breathed out by
Black Angus behind the fence

AUGUST

Dream your dreams my little mother
dance your dance, sing again your story

Tonight, darkness rolls up, over and under.
One dark sphere contained within itself,
around me, around all of us held safely
by the hands of Gaia. From the lake,
I hear the water roll up, over and under
contained within this sphere of night.
Below the water, creatures grow and change
roll within their shells, within this water
within this darkness, within the hands of Gaia.

One by one, mitochondria begin slowly to see
to hear, and then to dream. Dream light
surrounded by darkness, surrounded by water.
Within this dream, they grow arms, legs
mouths, sing dreams of water sky and clouds
dance slowly from water to land between
darkness and light within the hands of Gaia

Dance your dreams my little mother
Sing again fourscore and five your story

Tonight I sit on my mother's porch
alone in her house, the old ghosts brush
against me. There are no stars this night
Four paper butterflies mark porch screens
Outside, insects catapult into the yard light
Trucks, buses, and cars brake and accelerate
horns blare half a mile east on the highway

Each time I visit, there are fewer items
Three weeks ago, I left with opals from
Australia, an eighty-year-old saxophone in the
key of C, and Uncle Bart's typewriter. This

time the trunk of my car is packed with
a decade of magazines and *Readers' Digest
Condensed Books*.

From her hospital bed, our mother rules
her kingdom by telephone. "When you come,
bring me toilet paper, tissue, socks, nice
underwear, my magnifying mirror, Aunt Marie's
shawl, and the magnifying glass." Only a week
ago she was taken to the doctor and put
directly into the hospital, so weak she
could not even whisper.

Within a four state radius, we telephone,
struggle through discussions with social workers,
nurses, health care providers. Mother announces
clearly what she will not do. Within these
bounds, within this family, within the light
and dark, we hold each other close, a sphere
of women. In darkness we reach for the
hands of Gaia. Lake and darkness roll over
and through each other again and again.

Dream on little mother, dream deep and swim
swim into the story of your song.

1988

Someday I will rise and go
where land is flat
trees old and few
enough for shade and birds
where sky changes quick
as the sea and storms roll
up and over mountains
made from clouds

There my house has eleven rooms
windows easily open for wind
white curtains blow ghosts
in and out of each room
just before a summer storm
stairs go up and stairs go down
a bannister with a newell post
all wood shows age and growth
mar of knotholes now and again

Basement shelves slowly
fill at the end of summer
jewels against winter:
green beans, gold corn
tomatoes, beets, peaches
a cotton line stretches
back and forth
winter wash brought in frozen
before noon

Red geraniums in the kitchen
rocking chair, grey tabby cat
wall of windows faces east
study each sunrise
until day opens the blue wall
of morning glories
fifty goldfinches
fill the apple tree

Wrap a porch around this house
high enough so puppies
and small children play
underneath in the cool dusk
July and August afternoons

Beyond the porch
blue columbine, poppies
yellow roses, wisteria
twists and climbs
touches the window
of each bedroom
summer nights sleepers
dream purple shadows
broken only by the
sharp crescent of
a strawberry moon

Tulips, peonies
Dutch iris, dwarf iris
daffodils, small purple
hyacinths, a blue sea
of spring scilla,
violets and dandelions

Phlox and sweet william
babies breath, moonflowers
and a month of lilacs
turk's-cap lilies
flax and lavendar
balloon flowers
blue and white
three apple trees
a weeping willow
wrens' song billows
sheets on the line

Each bed wears a quilt
cut from pieces of our lives

we sleep on pillows
filled with down
curl and uncurl
in our attic bed
wake and listen
sleep again

There is one more room
I have stayed away
it is yours, large as you like
windows where you will
room for your thoughts
books and words
hopes and dreams

I sit and spin
in a turret
come find me
open the door
climb the stair
watch hawks circle
wait for rain
and the smell of sage

OCTOBER 27, 1994

I answer the phone
our youngest son rasps
"Mom, Dad is dead.
Breath, smile, bones vanish.

Our youngest son,
born early, his sternum
still undone, born so small
I couldn't hold him
raced to an incubator
this son named twice
for you chokes
"Mom, Dad is dead."

Five weeks ago you slept
your white hair wings
around your head
your face almost radiant
asleep easy as a child
the oxygen line
as much a part
as your toenail
I wanted love
and prayer to cure
lungs, heart,
and hurt.

I leave
drive into the dark
know our son drives
in more darkness
hopes to find us
somewhere together
beyond this night.
Later, I hold him
tight before he moves
away to breathe

in and out, count
breaths as Avés.

Thirty-one years
we shared two sons
four houses, three cars
cats, confusion over
money, relatives
each other, our sons
a number of dogs
Civil Rights, Vatican II.

Our youngest son and I
buy the best suit
you ever wore
his first suit
and black shoes.
We call those few
who really knew
select a casket
bury you.

Our oldest son calls
"I can't believe
I'll never talk
to Dad again."
He'll talk
to the coroner
arrange for the
RV to be returned
create ceremonies
to say good-bye.

Our youngest says
"I hear Dad say
'Go back to school.
Get all As.' "
They reach for
each other and me
I open my arms.

ACROSS THE STREET

October everywhere. Blue jays carry sky blue as
the last cornflowers in the garden. Mums burst gold,
rust, white below maple trees bright enough to break
your heart. Along the river, cottonwood leaves strum
the end of summer while waves of blackbirds write their
music across the sky.

Ben and I, old neighbors, wave across the street. His
step, twenty years more spry than yesterday. He waves
his cane. I cross the street. Now that he can't garden
anymore, his fingernails and shoes are always clean. We
sit on the chairs in front of his brown house.

"Something happened last night that I can't tell you,"
he says. "But I feel a lot better. I feel like I'm
sixty again."

He settles back, closes his eyes, and drifts a moment.
"I dreamed I waltzed with an angel. I used to like to
waltz. We were dancing to music. I never heard music
like that. No, I never heard music like that. She
was dressed all in white, and we were waltzing."

He shakes himself a little and opens his eyes. "I
woke up. Everything was gone. I was mad. I never
heard music like that."

He looks at me, his old eyes blue as today's sky. Then,
he gets up, takes his cane, and we both walk through
the remnants of his raspberry patch. "I feel better
today. Gee, I was mad. I feel like I'm sixty again."

Above our heads the blackbirds soar a crescendo, turn
and glide a diminuendo, the cottonwoods continue their
syncopation.

SUSAN THURSTON HAMERSKI

RIDING FAST IN THE PICKUP OVER ROLLING ROADS

My stomach lifts into my throat
along with the words
do it again
Father laughs
at the idea of his youngest
giving permission
to drive fast very fast
over the rolling
township road
on our way home
from the swimming hole
Outside there is yellow dust
small stones hop like
grasshoppers from beneath the tires
My brothers and I are aligned
on the bench seat as he presses
the pedal down, tells us
don't breathe a word
of this to your mother
and for a Chevy-pickup moment
we inhabit a bluebird
our bones light with summer
with not doing the right thing
And we do not worry about the clouds
gathering in the west
about to tumble hail
and straight-line winds
through our wind-rowed hearts.

MY MOTHER'S BODY

The egg cracked while boiling.
Pressure pushed white scalding
insides out. I peel the shell
from the soft seam like blanched lips
pursing up from sphered and smooth
near-perfection. Like your
scar, an angry smile beneath the breast
where your cancer was scraped out.

We stand and walk in mother
daughter rhythm; my body
wrapped in younger skin
mimics yours. We are full
and voluptuous, with a mutual
hate of heat. We knock
against each other, surfaces
crack, and we blister.

Your scar is a seam upon my fear:
will this be part of your body's
legacy? I look at my naked self.
My breasts hold dependable shape
are lifted only by gentle hands, nothing
more than pleasure expected from them, not
warm milk or suspicious tissue.
Today I am heavy with unpierced eggs.

MOON WALK

For weeks I watch and hope, wait for the seeds
to lift something Greek and green from their terra-cotta
circle. Stolen seeds, taken from a Delphic breeze, as if
the Oracle blew them into my hand. Again this morning
I offer them a light watering, an oblation of the eye,
then return to the newspaper where I am reminded
today is the anniversary of the first moon landing.

Just before my tenth birthday. Warm summer.
The television filled with black and white madness.
Few heroes walked the earth.
My thighs sweat on the green Naugahyde
ottoman. I watched the moon's surface delivered
into the living room, a vast beach in search of a sea,
a ruin of a god's imagination.
Marshmallow men lifted rocks light as seeds to bring home.

On Earth the ignorant and romantic believed
remnants of suspended secrets slept in those rocks.
Brought back to laboratories and great expectations,
they did not bloom. Nothing is as sinister
as science without a story. Again I examine the seeds,
search for island disturbances, germinating moons.
But these seeds refuse me. I am in need of a more fertile magic.

STREET CONSTRUCTION

They will   never finish
will always   be digging
deeper   never satisfied
even after tearing
below the frostline where storm sewer
and catalpa roots rest in a comfort not easily afforded
this far north   never offered
without a price. Nothing
under this   never street
knows the color blue.

I stand next to piles of centenary fragments
mounds resembling earth
but more forgotten
and recognize nothing.
When all is dislocated I begin naming:
here is   window frame
here are   wooden steps
here is   boulder where children safe from war
stop to sit and eat licorice before making their way home.

I let out the dog. She runs, feels the air change
as if she knows Thursday the moon will swell into harvest
heaviness. I turn from street construction and see
delphinium. Even from here the last stalks shake
wonders at me. Soft white pistils like butterfly teeth.
Doubled, veined blue calyx upon plum corolla.

Blue has not been stripped from this place. Not yet.
I cut one stalk
long on stem
bring it indoors
give it warm water
second breath
and in its milk glass vase
a new surface to rest against
an interior season.

THESE ARE MY IMAGININGS, FOR ALL YOU TOLD ME
WAS I WENT DAYDREAMING IN THE CORN FIELD

In the corn field amidst harvest you move with the certainty of
ownership and again you realize how much you miss the place
how it never really can be left this field this land upon which
you raised children and hopes you pick the corn wrapped as if
it were some exotic sweet in gold tissue kernels even and hard
as teeth determined to fulfill a covenant you are glad for the
stubborn seed your mind like the wind races over the children
the grandchildren surrounds you with leaf tongued clacking
and you want to hear another voice amidst the rows so you
listen hard for the tasseled rustle of his voice and for a time you
can pretend he is not dead but simply waiting for you to walk
deep into the field to take an ear of corn and remember how it
felt to hold such promise in your hand to touch it like fine sweet
pearls and remember your youth and then the wind shifts and
there is someone else who moves among the rows and you
know it is that woman that entire other life that could have been
you the one you tried to hide who seemed always to roll images
near your periphery like sunlight through cornstalks and this
time you do not avoid her and must account for your choices
this is where I cannot follow you even in a poem as much as I
want to know everything about you there are some things a
daughter should not imagine about her mother so I leave you
two alone to share secrets as you leave me to mine and later I
imagine you as you leave the field and scramble up the ditch
dragging a sack of corn with you and you do not look back.

FOR THE AUTUMN THAW

This is what can catch you unawares. You expect
winter. Deep freeze. Solid ground. Deep sleep. Then

warmth. A warmth that sends melting snow rushing
at toboggan speed down slate shingles. That drives

icicles like gossip-charged tongues into the ground.
This is not an internal spring warming. This thaw's

source is external. You cannot work a little harder,
break a sweat, force it in any way. It is irresistible.

As easy as an embrace. As expected and terrifying
as a recurring dream. More than a splendid wish,

it is requited passion. This is a gentle virus you
hope will invest itself into every cell. The earth

softens into a surprised mud that sucks at your boots
as if it wants to strip you of all your dull wool garments.

This is what it means to be the beloved, as if you are cloaked
in medieval tapestry where real gold rises from the fire.

And you are satisfied with courtly, long fingers
that knead the string of knots you call your back

into a velvet ladder. This lover is a collector of warm days, can
hold winter in mid-step, keeps that certain silencer

from entering your heart a little while longer. Then one night
while you are walking beneath the full moon

following your large shadows, you turn your face into a cold
wind. The thaw retreats. You enter your winter

house, alone with the effort of keeping warm. And the thaw
paces in its eternal August room, watching your life.

MOURNING

Warm and washed clean of the blood
denied its purpose, you are home.

You touch the silk of your
skin and reach to grasp the heat
of his; in sorrow he
sleeps wrapped around you.

In a dream, you cut portions of your
self away, the best parts from the two
of you, and mold the slippery
shining flesh into a tight and perfect

Pill. You swallow it and it falls
into the hollow bulb within you.
This seed settles into the comfort
of your red dark space.

Fired with your passion, rich
with salt from your tears, this
time the cells hold tight and strong
divide, curl, spiral into that infinite

Dance we all know. It becomes a lyric
inside, knocking and rolling
around in your most intimate home. You
swell, glimmer, and deliver the creation

Who is greater than both of you. People call it
a miracle, but it is much more. Dreams can be like that.

LIONS IN THE GRASS

It takes four quarts of dandelion blossoms to make
A gallon of wine. Just the blossoms. No stems.
Absolutely no greens. Not even the star-shaped cup
Rocking the yellow puff. Greens spoil the flavor.

I want to turn the abundant weed into a respected
Flower. Want to bottle a golden, sweet essence
Holding time. At least early summer. A liquid
Reminder of our first year here in this home.

I snap the caps into my palm. Fill the pail.
Let the stem-milk stain my fingers mud-yellow.
At the sink, I watch an oriole dip in the freshened
Water of the bird bath as if it were sugar. I pluck
The center of the blossoms. Soft as baby chick feathers.

My first sip of alcohol was Grandma's dandelion wine.
The last of it drunk long ago, with aunts, uncles,
Cousins at Thanksgiving. Warm wine so good I
Ached for adulthood. I want to be as determined as Grandma.
Pluck enough blossoms; peel away bitterness.

I remember Mother telling Grandma
She starts everything and finishes nothing.
Not true. I finish many things. Books. Work days.
Poems. Arguments. I can forever stroke the back of a dog,
Lift to love making motion, creak in a porch swing
On an August night. It's not that I don't finish,
I just cannot leave things alone.

But right now I can no longer tolerate blossom plucking
Tedium. I suspect Grandma's five children did the blossom
Work. She would have commanded such child-slave love-
Labor. The wine recipe book also has a rhubarb scheme.
Red stalks and green elephant ears of leaves grow dense
In a patch out back. Four quarts of one-inch pieces.
No plucking.

LEARNING TO DIVE

The lake cleans house; three-foot waves
lift and release driftwood, rocks,
dead creatures, from iced suspension.
Shoreline birch cradle waiting buds.
All morning, four male red crested mergansers
encircle and entreat a ruddy headed female.
At last she chooses. Or gives up.
Now in mated shadow two
move over the lake's surface
already easy with each other
diving into the waves.

Nearby, two boys and one
little girl play
on the rock shelf.
I watch as she
colt-legged
scales the same rocks
as her older brothers.
She manages, barely.
They do not check her
don't seem to care that she
wants to be
with them.
She reaches out
as if to embrace the waves
and I am there
inside her
want the waves
to be big
and loud
want them
to wash the boys away
leave her standing.
Her parents will ask
in horror

Where are your brothers?
And she will shake out her
wet hair and say
I tried to warn them
but they wouldn't listen.
The waves crash near her feet.
Touch no one.

We are good at this pairing.
We are good even
when we're bad.
It is Wednesday night
date night my mother called it.
We eat crab with our bare hands
fingers poke and push
out every sweet shred.
We suck butter-soaked
garlic cloves that pop
like warm grapes in the mouth.
We spread the over-cooked
artichokes into moon-lotus centerpieces.
We play the dusted-off
Benny Goodman and Glen Miller tapes
again and again and we dance
foxtrot, Lindy, our invented steps.
It is so hot, but we feed
another log to the fire
want this heat
and the open window
through which we can
hear the waves crashing.
We dive into all of this.
We think of our parents
who danced to these same songs
who drank a little too much sometimes
who listened to the sound of waves
and liked to feel so hot
after such a long winter.

SIGI LEONHARD

LIKE ONE BODY

I. First Night

Every night is the first night.
I wake up from a faint cry.
She lies on her side the way
She fell asleep after nursing.
I have never seen anyone so small
Look me straight in the eyes
As if to say, and who are you? Except
Our gaze met not in the realm of words
And sentences.

I say: Eyebrows wrinkled,
She looked at me skeptically. I say:
Like a lover, yes, searching
My face for signs
Only she could decipher.
Our eyes so close we saw
Each other's face distorted, picasso-like
The right half higher than the left,
And I get high on the night sky
Of her eyes
That looked at me like those
Of a sage from a distance.

But behind all the images
Invented to preserve those seconds
In a medallion of words,
The first night fades,
And I say no to the pictures
Of skeptic and lover
And the sage and eyes like a night sky.
No, ours was a landscape
Of freshly fallen snow
At dawn, no footprints had left
A message on the place where our eyes met.

Ours was a world of blurry flakes, falling so slowly
As to make light of gravity.
And now, many nights later, my pen
Walks across that field and gives a place
To "snow" and "field" and
Sets its meanings like monuments
To a time before words. We call it a march
Of language against forgetting, but I say
Ours was a world of no set phrases, no meanings
Baked hard in the oven of language, only
The melting of our eyes
In a never-before and a never-again
And the always of that
First night.

II. Solstice

When the days started
To get longer
We made her

Or rather
She came to us
Because we asked for her

Or rather
We weren't sure at all
Whether we wanted

Her or the old life
That was after all comfortable
Or if not comfortable at least

Known. But we didn't know
It would actually happen
When we made her

She made us into something
We hadn't been before

Or rather some one or some
Thing immaterial beyond our acts of In-
Decision stepped in and acted. I

Now think of us as the channels
Through which she came
Think of what called her as a will beyond ours

Or rather
A great joy that wanted to see her laugh
And dance trampling on the bed

Like the spirit of life itself.

III. Christmas

A year ago she lay in her car seat
Under the Christmas tree. I didn't know
How to be a mother. Her father ran around
With the video camera he had bought
For her arrival. He filmed her everywhere:
On the kitchen table, in the basket near
The washing machine, in his bed, so small
He could finally put the zoom to use,
On my arms, and, of course,
Under the Christmas tree where she lay
Blinking at the lights. Was she dazzled? Scared?
We knew she was incredibly developed
For her three months.
We carried her through the house in the attempt
To make her understand Christmas and to make her feel
At home. Later, when I looked at the video, I saw
Two frantic adults running up and down the stairs
And an infant, smiling in the direction
Where the excited voices came from,
To the left, to the right and once in a while upwards,
Towards the Christmas tree.

IV. The Blueprint of Mystery

The facts are known. From the blastocyst's
Glob of cells to the photograph of the child at seven months
Shielding her eyes from the intrusive light
Of reason and medical intervention,
We can see her now
As God sees her: curled around her own mystery,
In her cosmic space. Her fine bones
Shine through the skin, she is still
More idea than matter, and yet
Everything is already there. We know
Down to the week when the spine forms,
When the eyes develop, when the eyelids
Close over them for a few months, and that,
In the latest part of pregnancy, the child can open
And close them at will. We know
That at seven months the nervous system
Is basically in place, and that there is reason
To believe the pianist who could play difficult pieces
On sight that his mother had practiced
While she carried him. There is reason to believe
The child can remember the sound of voices
And feel whether she is being bounced around
In joyful expectation or angrily.
We can see the blueprint of mystery
And decide, every day, what will
Become of it.

> *Don't think of your toddler as a big baby;*
> *think of her as a short adolescent.*

V. The Fit

Her father calls it demented rage.
She hurls herself onto the floor as I pull
The garbage can out of her hands
And the potato peels which she is determined
To eat. I call it a bad day because

She woke up early from her nap,
But my words drown in a high-pitched
Fury of screams. I never knew
Of a scream that scrapes your ear drums.
Her father tries to enunciate the firm
But not uncaring "No" that is supposed
To set boundaries. I hold her
With my arms stretched out
So she can't hit me
Or herself.

If it isn't one thing, it's another. I see
Her point only too well. We are
No fun. We shove ourselves
Between her and the world: No
To hitting the cat. No
To the interesting food
In the garbage can. No to the smooth
Mirror of water in the toilet bowl
In which you can rinse Dad's toothbrush.
No to eating the catfood.

She calms down. She has seen
Mom's engagement calendar
Under the highchair, and hurries
To get it before the next "No."
Like a dilettante thief, she runs
Into her favorite corner, opens it,
Looks at the pages with an earnest face
And gets to work.

We look at each other
And pretend we haven't noticed.
During a blissfully quiet
Half hour, with a cup of coffee
And the Sunday paper for us,
She rips out a few pages
Of March, then of August,
And hides them
Under the frying pan.

VI. Like One Body

When she needs me at night
I run to her room barefoot
My eyes half closed
At two a.m. I pick her up   She
Wraps her legs around me   Knows
My waist and   How to ride
My hips   She knows that I
Will pick her up   Will carry her
To my room   To my bed   Will
Slide with her down
Onto the pillow   When she needs me
Late at night   She knows   And in
The corridor already   She stops crying
And puts her head into the space
Between my shoulder and my neck   I
Under the stern eye of the moon
Carry her   Eyes half closed and barefoot
And whisper   We are going now
To bed   To sleep   To dream together
At two   At three   At four a.m.
I never put her down   We sink
Onto the pillows like one body   And
Already she is back asleep   And I lie grateful
For a while   Then she sleeps easily
At two and three and four a.m.
And breathes warmth into my bed
And peace and sweetness
When she needs me late
At night.

STORIES FOR HEALING

I. Winter

Smoke rises from a chimney in the valley
The crows scream
The old garden gate stands stark against the snow
An airplane cuts the sky and a milky sun
Rests her hand on the bare branches of the oak

II. Winter Speaking

Leave it to the snow   Quietly
It eats its way into the doorframes whirls around
The fence sticks to its rusty wire
All is light under the moon
Of a clear night

It is time to leave the country of dreams
It is time to use everything according to its own nature
Watch the wood yield its dense youth
To heat and light   Listen to its song
Of transformation

Crows ascend into the sky with their outrage
Snow has buried the harvested fields   The deer
Withdraw deep into the woods   The willows' hair
Frozen to the edge of the pond dreams
A brittle dream about spring

Use everything   The heat of breath
Near your mouth   The foggy mornings
The streetlight circle at the intersection
After midnight when you walk the streets
Wrapped in animal skin towards the seed of a future
Hidden in the kernel of this night.

III. This Time of Year

It does not bother me to be awake at three-fifteen Sleep
Will return eventually I climb down the stairs
Without turning on the light and try to avoid the steps that creak
The most so I won't wake up the baby In the kitchen
The cat looks at me quizzically as I let the water pour
On a big towel He does not understand
Why I am in the kitchen now He does not know about dust
     allergies
That wake you up in the middle of the night sneezing
With a raw throat and I can see in his eyes the hope
Of an unexpected feeding Outside the fresh snow
Shines in the night You could read a book out there.
I think how in the winter we have short days but nights
So bright you don't need the lights I think
Standing there with my towel ready for the radiator
That it is all right this winter this cold this time
In a house never finished with windows that don't close right
And the old floors creaking and all appliances falling apart
     inexplicably
After a short time I look out at the night sky and it is all right
     now
The hardship of this winter The trees breathe
An acceptance written faintly into the stars There is peace
In the motionless silence of the night I talk to the cat
And we both look out at the snow We know
Tomorrow will not be quite as cold as today and we will go out
He to hunt squirrels I to walk through the snow and remember
The scroll of the night sky We know
More snow will fall tomorrow
And in a week the days will be getting longer

IV. Stories for Healing

What we don't have
Is the magic carpet
Airy but indestructible
Solid but made
From light weight enigma

At five-thirty
The night is
For all practical purposes
Over

In the doorframe
With the baby on one arm
And the newspaper under the other
I glance at the world's latest
Disasters

Starving children and corpses
Before breakfast
What have we not stomached?
The highjacked plane burnt out
And the serial murderer
Who says he realizes
That he went too far

Where are the stories for healing?
The magic carpet disappears
From the children's books
When they are old enough
To read

Still I try
To make this life sturdy
And colorful
A fabric that will hold
The child and me and a few
Others

The cup of tea when
In my body the night
Is anything but over
The cat's balancing act
On my window sill
The milky flower
As we breathe
On winter's window—

Threads in the carpet
Of hope—

It is a terrible moment
To realize
Your mouth is eating a muffin
While your eyes take in
The headlines and the picture
Of a blood-covered child

But who could go on
Without moments of comfort
And not forget
That the day is created
Each morning
For joy and amazement
And grace

JOANNE MAKELA

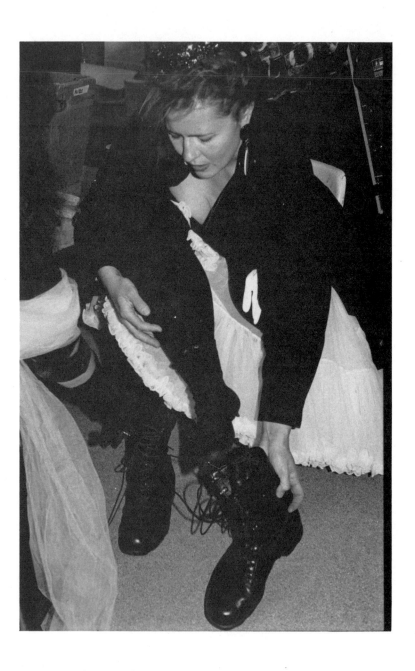

LAND WIFERY

I come from thick-soled people
  who crossed the frozen land bridge
  over the Bering Sea

Solitary nomads
  hunted caribou, reindeer
  on icy steppes

Fat was is an asset
Girth is was worth

I worship and honor in sexualritual
  the hunting mother
  her fertility has no calendar
  her ground is always ready
  to nourish seed

She cannot rely on the timely
  efforts of sun
  the welcoming nature of earth

Death lies below the permafrost
She is the only warm home
any future will ever know.

WANT

My friends will shame me
into saying I
am in love. It is
not true. There is no
warmth to this feeling, just
despair, hunger, pain,
curiosity.
It does not have the homeliness of good
bread and wine. It is
hot pepper burning
the tongue. It will not
quench with water. Thicker
substances are needed.
Blood surges, rages
in tidal wave,
forcing reason through
windows and cracks in
the surface. It is
passion, lust and greed—
that hunger for which
there is no other meal.

CARTESIAN THEORY

My philosopher says
when I am not with you
you are not there

yet there you are
swimming my depths
a fish seeking sun

teasing me with your wiggling bait
whispering between my legs
the secret combination
to my master lock

sprung
a rusty hinge the only thing
between me and life

Your breath in my ear
your scent in my hair
your lips nursing my breasts
coaxing my secret places
back
back
back
up
up
up

into light
gasping air
I break from my dark wet prison
from the sharp edges of debt

we die again
we live again
motionless

we change anyway
we change despite ourselves

Your voice lives in the shofar I lift to my mouth
in the cup from which I drink
your voice speaks of change
anesthetized
remote
your voice sounds in your own head
so you cannot hear it
you speak to me in tongues
only I understand

My hands live in your back pocket
they climb fences
push bacon
knead the bread of you
pinch the salt of you
form the biscuit of you
exchange the ball of desire between them
slice boundaries
scratch patterns remembered by only them

I am whelmed by you
welcomed into your mouth
into your bed
into your kitchen

sautéed in your juices
I bathe away
obsession
that death that picks apart
the object of desire
bit by bit
until the object is left thin
scraped bare
and obsession is made fat.

SLEEP NAKED (WANT 2)

What I want is the want

I want the want
the me in it
I want that moment when you see me
in my genie outfit
that moment that screams
I want you
I want that genie in my bottle
out of her bottle
on my bottle neck

I want the desire that lets you sleep naked with a stranger

no thought of could, would, should

the same want that inspires you to say
I want to suck your toes
do something fun to me

want doesn't want nice
no competition to use the word first

When I want you want me
I'm there on top of you
When I don't want you don't want me
I go away

as simple
as pure
as sane
as that.

BONE LION

In this dream she has long hair
and eyes gold, both gold, both glow in the dark
she takes his hand
he can feel her bones
no flesh, she is transparent
they walk into the jungle
an old woman sits on a rock
her hair a wild mane that forms a halo around her face
her eyes are always closed
they kneel in front of her
offer her fruit and flowers
but she wants meat
she takes the man into her arms as if he were a child
she cuddles him and soothes him
begins to eat him gently
he doesn't stir
when she is done eating
her flesh falls away from her body
she is all bone
her eyes open
they glow like coals
she tilts back her head and roars

HER BODY A XYLOPHONE

she hums with certain
vibration
hollow sound
mallets on bone
up and down
the rib cage
tinkling ivory
thunk and ring
her spine a curvature
of music
its atonal quality
resonates solidly in the room
an acoustic perfection
not met by mortal creations
she lifts her black dress
shows an undulating
skeleton
behind the dark drape
a symphony of corporeal
instruments
the conductor lifts a
finger baton

HIDDEN AGENDA

There is a long way between you and me
a mountain
a jungle
a war
a diametric opposition.

Still, our arms reach out
our fingers clasp
our lips touch
fleetingly
longing for one more push
an electric malfunction
a guard asleep at the gates.

We migrate and make do
make due
make love
like strangers with strangers
looking for someone lost.

Our children are ourselves
we pamper them
feed them too much
smother them with wool blankets.

In finding me you lose me every time.

THE ART OF REMEMBERING

She begins to forget touch
and love
what love feels like
what it feels like to be loved
what she loved about touch

tactile sensations seize
her hands go numb
then her thighs
soon she cannot walk on her rubber legs

they say the body can shut down its parts
in extreme circumstances
the body protects itself from extreme pain
the body triggers the mind with chemicals
and alters state of being

some inherited prophylactic unsheathes itself
over the injured part

in her case
those parts that touch
the skin
the lips
the hair
the digits
the extremities

all shut down
to avoid the pain
the loss of the hands that touched them
the other that reached them
in love and in violence
her electric connection to the world

she exists as an isotope
a free radical
missing a complement
she floats in ionic space.

THE ART OF LETTING GO

Gradually she has learned to let go of things
still, she will not admit defeat

she walks him slowly through her life
their life together
in one sense—the flicker of an eye
in another—an eternity

he does not want to look as she points out her pain
here and here
he could never look at her pain
so she learned to lie about it
here and here

this made her dishonest
untrustworthy
a shifter

she takes tiny, mincing steps
through the agony
and small joys

as they pass these things
they are releases
tiny gasps of letting go
small orgasms
let them ride the wave back to the starting point

here and here

she has another walk to make.

RIKI KÖLBL NELSON

PAPER-WHITES IN JANUARY

From underground
tessellated
pale green hoods
poke stiff little tongues
through brown layers of skin
sticking it to old man winter
From the puckered onion
half underground—
that balled fist
holding back
just enough to sustain a slow
unfolding
of what it has known
and will show us
again and again:
how to go with the sun
elongate
unfold   stretch   stay connected
open up and give out

BEING SMALL   BEING A GIRL

I. The geese would come at her the moment she went into the yarc
    What could they detect?
    Eye level with her, wings wide, long necks stretched forward
    they would come.
    Beaks as if to strike, hissing.
    Necks wavering like snakes.
    Eyes close to the top of their heads—
    like bald men intent on evil.

    Being small. Being a girl. Having to be neat.
    Stitching with a needle on paper, following lines.
    Wearing pinafores.
    Finger paint nowhere on the horizon.
    No mess.

    Sent to the cellar with the coal bucket she scampered in fright.
    So black and cold—pit of nightmares, away from the upper
    world of kitchen smells and squabble, tea on the stove,
    mother's sewing machine humming
    She would hold her breath
    shovel the coals quickly, scooping up as much as
    she could in the bucket. Not enough light.
    Fear creeping from the unlit corners as if all the untold sorrows
    had seeped down moaning their low tune.

II. In first grade, maroon-dyed tights.
    Everyone else wore beige or brown, white on Sunday.
    She hated those tights.

    The wrong boy in school liked her, even said hello
    to her when she was out with her parents
    on the obligatory Sunday afternoon walk. She pretended
    not to hear, but her parents nudged her, smiled.
    They thought he was sweet.

    She remembers sitting over her sketch book
    in the kitchen drawing, going into a different world.
    Praised for her results, she was told that it was the same

talent her grandfather had—
the grandfather she could not remember.

III. The circus. Big crowd. Animal dung.
Dancer on slim legs. Magic. Grace.
The small second floor apartment where they lived
had a balcony. Its floor a foot above
a smooth tin roof over the blacksmith's below.
Her stage. She climbed over the railing.
She was the dancer.

Often she wore a gold-colored charm, a running horse
on a chain around her neck. One day on her way
home from nursery school she dawdled, went down
to the brook that ran through the village.
Played. Bent down in the mud.
The chain broke.
The little horse almost lost in the water.
Her older sister rescued it.
Still they were scolded.

IV. She dreams.
Small, she walks along
the edge of the wood. Two black
bears come toward her, huge, menacing.
She knows they will tear her to pieces.
Needs to run back into the garden through
the huge door and into the house. She turns, looks over
her shoulder, feels their rank breath. Just
then she splits in two: a white horse that runs
screaming with wild eyes and gets away
and a girl who cannot run fast enough.
The bears are upon her. She wakes—
the scream rings in her ear.

V. The mature woman sings to the small girl. Sings
peace. Sings belonging. Sings mine.
She takes the child's hand. They run
hard and fast, soles coming down with a clap. Faster
and faster. Laughter in their chests spilling
out like water over the rim of a baroque fountain.

BELUGAS

At the aquarium
they curve their big heads
Their calm eyes
lean to us
They hold us
in silent communion
tenderly
Not one iota of malice
in the big house of their soul

In the valleys of the deep
they sing whole epics
each tribe its own watery song
repetitions
rhymes
for their memory
They tell of greens and blues
thalo, cerulean, ultramarine
of ships hidden in coral
shadowed by fish

Their dreams are rounded
and curved
In their bellies we would hear their song
from the inside out

TRANSITION

It's the summer of shorts and play pants
the summer I still run topless
in the fenced-in garden
full of currant and gooseberry bushes

At home in my body
I like how it moves
I like its sweat
A good horse
it knows what I want
the moment I want it

It's the summer of long limbs
and monkey grace
as I curl my leg over
the gray iron bar next to the poles
holding up the swing
I can do knee-waves
and back-flips
touch the ground and go back up
I never get dizzy
my grip prehensile, tight
When I take a break for snacks
I taste metal from my hot palms

This is my bar, my place of skill
One sister a sissy
the other too small
I share only with friends   Taking turns
we compete, watch with tight eyes

One day
I roll and roll
ride my knee-waves
but something bucks
All of a sudden

I am flat on the ground
eyes opening on the point of a pine tree—
green cross held in the sky
I don't know what happened
but things changed in the fall

LAUGHING

I.   I go under
    This is the Ur-place
    this green pond in the crater
    There are calcium formations
    miniature Aztec terraces
    diminishing, tapering down

    I recognize the call in the other language
    My sisters are waiting
    We link hands voicelessly laughing
    dancing the slowest round, languid
    our long hair making lazy tendrils
    We look almost alike
    we are three and yet one
    We know secrects
    and sometimes
    the water birds learn them from us

II.   I want to dance nude
    Einstein hiding in the trees
    Come on old goat! I say
    twinkle my moon at him
    eyes over my shoulder
    run, splash
    lie on my back, float
    Leave the sad-eyed
    goat in the sand
    The sun is enough
    glad skin awash
    belly-easy on the waves

    I want to cross
    hip-high fields in sunlight
    sit on the fence
    shout HA!
    Be loud, guffaw, whoop
    say what I mean
    and say it clear

DREAM DELPHINIUM, LARKSPUR

Standing on the ground floor
my back to five oblong windows reaching down
branches, leaves almost touching the glass
from outside
green shadiness, cool
with pockets of sunlight
as if under water
the woods coming up to the round house—
my own house

Standing on the wooden floor
flecks of light dancing across
I face the round table
gold, umber
teak, and light walnut—
I think of the times I was cruel

A burst of blue and lilac
like many arms waving welcome—
flowers my dead mother has put
in a vase for me
delphinium, larkspur
lilac primrose of the swampy
meadow we called little chicken eyes
We picked them for Mother's Day
Brought them home in warm fists

But these have faces large as carnations
They radiate
All I can do is stand there
and think how these flowers must mean
she forgives.

WITH THIS RING

Oma gave me this ring to use in my wedding
that June many years ago
Students just out of graduate school
we had a small wedding in Falls Church with
silver friendship rings, another in Austria
Two weddings, one in each country
less paperwork, less red tape, but
more family. We did not want
to spend money on traditional rings
Oma said, I have two. You can use my gold
wedding band and my mother's
There was only the one band from her own
wedding, the other one lost, gone because
Opa had been taken from their house and put
into a camp. We don't know precisely when or
how he died or where he was buried, whether
alone or in a mass grave. Or what they did
with his ring. I am sure it was
taken off—personal loot, or clumped
together in a pile of rings.

My sister Christl said she was taken aback
when our father took my mother's wedding
band off her finger after they had washed her body
and dressed her, before she was carried out. He put a rose
from the garden into her hand and said, Good-bye Friederl
Months earlier she had divided her jewelry
into three large groups, one for each daughter
small piles for her two granddaughters, earrings, pins, rings.

I WANT

for you to buy me back telling me you can't
live without my big butt, my full lips, lumpy
thighs, the gap between my teeth, the scar
low on the right side of my belly, the other
one, a long zipper on my back plus the small
one almost imperceptible below my jaw and
the very new one curving under my right
nipple—these imperfections, my trophies
of living, surviving

buy me back with glances that say I count,
claim me with looks far across the room over
the heads of women younger, of firmer flesh
different promises

buy me back with all the flowers I want over
and over, the diamond ring I thought I didn't
need but long for, buy me with low
whispers, eyes of desire, heart as hungry as
mine

HOLDING OUT

Daily I read
cornfields
touched by frost
tawny gold
light after bearing
I see rustling

Green lingers
in fields
and roadsides
boosts the rust
of sorrel and thistle

Most oaks
declare stark limbs
but some
spell burgundy
A few aspens
in gold
hold out

In gentle hollows
sumac sleeps
umber alizarin
subdued crimson
juice holds color
into the wind
this is a prime season
a full-throated hum
of having known
knowing
still wanting more

MARCELLA TAYLOR

RESUMING THE JOURNEY

I loved sitting there
at only a slight distance
from those slender bay windows,
the huge elm tree outside
brushing against brownstone walls.
Moses, the middle cat,
would perch on the window seat
watching squirrels and birds
in a rare moment of contentment.

I made a space inside me
for that shelter, its elegant white walls,
spotless marble fixtures, high
ceilings, gallery lights. I liked
its flow of open spaces, the sun
entering and travelling
from one corner to another
unimpeded. The cats rolled across
carpets together, forming dual
and triple bonds. At times,
I felt like an outsider.

Even there. I let those light-
filled rooms in but kept
myself out, wandering from
day to day as if in a convoluted
tunnel, waiting
for a point of arrival.

I wrote in my journal.
*I will make these spaces my own
when I discard alien alliances,
the only fruit
of a beleaguered life.*
This place that touched my being
I could not own
for I did not own myself.

I sold it to a couple
who would divide their time
between this city place
and a river house, who
in that division
would weld body and space.

I packed the furniture
which fit only with great unease
into other rooms, bundled the cats
into carriers without bars.
We started on our way, moving
from place to place, their sustainment
the familiar smells of each other,
mine only the journey itself.

FLOWERS FOR CHARLIE

All in girlish white
I sat stiffly at a table
in the bar
not sure what to order.

You smiled
a handsome glint
in your blue eyes, ready
to follow my lead.

The other two settled
for beers, we dared the cocktail.
You were my first college date
and I was too young.

Why am I remembering you
tonight, decades later?
Is it the figure of my silence,
the awkwardness of my feet

the fear of showing
how proud I felt
to have been matched with
the catch of the college town?

The hall was a film
of floating shadows, the music
silenced
after our second dance

our midnight goodbyes
at the convent dorm tentative.
You were off to the army
and only now

with all the miles between
this room and the men
I still love, am I wondering
if you made it back alive.

TELEPHONE VOICE

When his voice
came over the wires

a voice I could no longer
pick out of a crowd

a voice of casual moments
swayed by the loveliness of leaves

the delicacy
of water and glass

when
through the passing of years

there came to me
the chord of remembrance

I turned back
not to that childhood solitude

lying on a porch
my back to the sappodilla tree

dreaming of a world I knew
could not exist

instead I recalled
how my body swelled and

needing more space began
to sweep a path this way and that

began to mail letters
without return addresses

began to lease rooms
without doors

when I heard cocooned in words
what the hand could hold

I made my body pause
still afraid

no matter what
it had just learned

I held my limbs still
not ready yet

to let the heart
explode.

ARCS

Now the pleasures come
not like the sun appearing
before the halt of rain
but like the first leaves of spring
expected, waited for
in painful emergence from the branch

or like the payday
with the money
already parceled out
the rent, the utilities
the half-empty
grocery bags.

Frantically, I shuffle the papers
layering my life, minutes
that hushed the excited cries
of childhood, the gold stars and badges
sucking in mildew
in some far recess of the body.

If joy has been squeezed
to a skeleton beneath the explosions
of life, if too many Roman candles
release only a fraction of their light
if the earth so filled with tremors
refuses these crescents

that will never become faces,
how can we learn to live
where both light and shadow frame us,
where our fingers cannot caress
the tops of the trees

how are we gifted to open
the door on our pain

in these weeks of birthing,
how let the tiniest color explode
full strength beneath our skins?

QUIET GATHERING

For a week with the family gone
I have tended the house,
cared for the things you love.

Out in the back garden, tomatoes
burden the vines. Ripened,
some now lie fallen, juices spilled.

I gather those still leaning
from the vine, the pale orange,
the clear red. In the picking,

they overflow my hands. I make
a basket of the front of my skirt,
carry them into the waiting kitchen.

I pick a golden-petalled flower, dark
center intact, a single bloom
to keep me company through the night

in this house filled with the harvest
that outlived you, this house
now too silent, this house of rest.

ROSEMARY, FOR REMEMBRANCE

Now, years after I heard no more
I recall less the garrulousness
of your body than
the ponderous motion of my hands
erecting glass walls. I hated
the erratic echo of your heels,
you struggling to catch up
with my lesser years. Your covered knees,
polyester jackets embarrassed me.

I flung my taut body to and fro
in bell bottoms, dark
peasant skirts, rust suede
that covered Twiggy hips. I slept
with more than one man, never
told you, feared you would not grasp
how that could be love.

Your ache for friendship
was a pungence, even in absence
always a part of the breath
of the world. I will never know
when your breathing ceased. Surgery,
a brain tumor, a faint scrawl
recording the hospital's number.

The image of a bouquet
eased in uninvited, strayed
to the corners of my heart.
All week, I trained my mind
in forgetting, hearing
the threat of broken glass
beneath my feet.

A fortnight later, I phoned
your house, a month later wrote

a letter, a year later
tried offices out of which you shared
your love for language
and for students. I fantasized
your face becoming vegetable,
a faceless brother visiting you
in some antiseptic cave.

It is many years now,
a cool August dawn. A raucous
birdsong tangles my brain.
An aged wind rises to remind me
of all I failed to do. I reach out
but to find the glass locked
in place. I must keep
these hands moving, fixed
on faces rising out of the dawn.

DAWN

I have waited long
for this day, the moment
when all would be less
tentative. This morning
the sun shines on everything
and we all know
that at last summer
has come to stay.

I too recognize
the recovered body
I will inhabit, the work
that will continue
through the years, the walls
that will enclose me,
the regrets that
will never desert me.

There is comfort in this,
finally learning how
to maneuver city traffic
without fear, no longer
reaching for cool lagoons
and steep mountains.

There is peace
in early wakings like this

and only the residue
of dreams sift
now and then
through my days.

BEVERLY
VOLDSETH

BEGINNING WITH HER

On her wedding night my mother had morning sickness, her
long skinny body already thickening, her parents quiet in the
rooms below. The bare yard reached out darkly from the white
house in moonlight; mulberry trees clustered near while the
plow disks, glinting wet from early dew, made a path to the
outhouse. Small, far buildings hunkered in shadow and to the
south the windmill creaked and clunked filling the round tank
where a girl not yet born would one day throw a chicken just to
see what it would do, her arms alive with its lice when she
rescued it. The barn loomed large and dense surrounded by a
pig-wire fence, the shuffling and snuffling of horses and pigs
held in by the blood-red boards. From there fields rolled out
and down the gullies to the dry creek bed where sixty summers
later a mass of yellow flowers would light up the hollow like a
fallen sun. On two sides the gravel road wrapped around fields
and farm place running off into the darker night past the small
schoolhouse, past the church, north to the big city where my
mother and father would soon move with their first child. I was
born fifth, all of us proof of the two year fertile cycle, except for
the seventh who waited three. Into that passivity, that silence
that would become my mother's existence, doing what needed
to be done without a word, I came needing words.

I am the dead child
gone to a far away land
where no one visits.
I hover outside my life
waiting for the realone
wondering who I am
wondering
doesheloveme
didshewantme
my coffin safe and comfortable

the graveyard small and quaint
I have lost my memory
and the loss consumes me
but I make no sign
ask no questions.
I remain the dead child
surrounded by a halo of dark

PHOTO OF A WOMAN WITH LONG HAIR

From some distant out-building, maybe the barn, but from
somewhere deep in his morning work he came, almost
from another country, so long had it been since anything like lust
had sparked between them. Or love. But she caught them both
unaware, she in the morning ritual of combing her hair, thinking
herself alone in that strange hour of day—everyone
out of the house—combed her thick and shining hair down
over her shoulder, over her left breast missing under her
best cotton dress, ran her strong fingers down over its length
past her waist. And then he came. For a handkerchief
he'd forgotten. For the notebook he didn't transfer into his clean
overalls the night before. Caught her there as he passed her door.
Came for his notes on chores and feed, his list, if he drove into
town, of what he might need. And when he caught her there,
her hand stroking the length of her hair, he said, Come.
Come out to the granary. Let me photograph your hair,
there where the elevator leans against the peak.
And because he caught her unaware she went.
Walked out over the dirt yard, past the summer kitchen,
past the tool shed. And because it had been a dry summer
gray dust puffed up around the soles of her black shoes.
Sun glinted off her glasses and she squinted as she
looked ahead at the distant elevator, the treeless space.
He placed her then, leaning slightly to the left,
her elbow on the conveyor, one foot behind the other.
She took her glasses off, dangled them in her left hand.
Maybe it was now she remembered they are not lovers anymore,
are not young. Closed her eyes, did not smile, but stood there
all the same (suffered it I want say), let him take a picture
of that black flame descending. And he remembering too
handed her the camera and walked toward the waiting wagon.

Or was it a daughter, eldest child of six who came upon her
mirrored in that backward stare, amazed by her mother's
unbound hair. Saw her as something other, then. Drew her
protesting outside into the sun. But why out past the summer
kitchen, the tool shed, to the idle elevator in front of the granary?

131

Why not to the front porch where she could have perched
on the railing, her arm around a post, her head leaning lightly
against the white. Everything in the picture white but the hair,
the black cascade down the front of her dress. Or if the sun
were too far gone, under the mulberry tree, lean her with her
hands behind her back against the trunk, stare her off into
the distance. Or at least against the white house at the corner.
Stand her near the boulder where so many pictures had been
taken of others. No, a daughter would not take her way out
to the granary.

Or did she herself walk, camera in hand, out to where the
tractor ran waiting to power the elevator, her husband and
the hired man, a child or two turning to stand in silence, to ˙
watch her as she came squinting at them in the sun. In front of
them at last, Here, she said, and thrust the camera into his idle
hand across the wooden frame of metal conveyors and chains.
Then, glasses dangling from her hand, rested her elbow on the
elevator's edge, and closed her eyes for that moment while the
camera clicked. She took the camera, flicked the dark mane
over her shoulder and walked back to the house. In her room
once more she closed the door, lifted scissors to her head
and whacked and whacked until all that black lay in clouds
upon the floor.

COUNTING

In the garden, hollyhocks higher than my head,
roses so bloomed as to be voluptuous,
the soil beneath my bare knees moist.
I count on my fingers
my dead.
Asters and zinnias nod
as if the list I recite quietly
aloud lived, and they are somehow privy.
I count.
I have my dead
but I am not sure I want to let them go.
The asters and zinnias nod some more.
They know that too.
Marigolds are expectant.
So count.
My knees are getting stiff;
legs won't hold me when I stand if I stay like this much longer.
My dead: Grandma, Grandpa, not in that order.
Both dead. All the other grands, all gone.
My father next. Aunt Mable, Uncle Henry, Uncle Chester.
Uncle Earl is now too, though he was dead to all of us
when he left Aunt Olga with four little ones, never came back.
Dead.
These are the easy ones, the long gone ones.
Most had separated from me or I from them so that dying
was the final but not the hardest separation.
Two babies of my own, one just a backache,
a clot of blood passed, the other tiny but already formed,
between my legs on the bed pad,
a small white center in a magenta blossom,
nurses bending over either side checking to see what was there.
I grieve them now, my sons, my boys too weak to live.
And there the list stops.
I ease over onto grass in a sitting position.
That's it.
Flowers press over the edges of their beds.

They are so beautiful; the fragrance in the morning air
enough to summon ecstasy.
I do not want to count anymore.
I let them all go once,
I do not want to let them go again.
Like the dried flowers I pull up
or cut down and put on the compost
the dead are all within me.
I have layered them around my heart.
They form a hard shell. I try not to count
too much on anyone again.

APTERYX

I am one of several flightless birds
       the only difference my longing

for flight

      such names
kiwi   ostrich   cassowary
      emu   moa

  exotic fruit on the tongue
  a language for lost love

to see
      their awkward bodies
the useless wings or none
      their ungainly attempts
          at motion

is to see the shape
        of my longing
   the impossibility of attainment

is to marvel
at
what we do to adapt

MANDALA WITH FIVE WORDS AND FOUR PARTS

If I could divide my world in four parts
contain it in a circle
a perfect circle with a strong rim
then all the hard things
would fall to the bottom
I could stand on them firmly
my feet spread for balance

the kingfisher diving at my arm
would miss me and get one of the fish
I did not draw but is swimming
somewhere behind me
I am not afraid

even though it is half dark
what is this yearning for water
to control the content of my life
wishing my body hairless
without blemish disowning
my father's moles my mother's whiskers
their varicose veins

even the moon is upside down
and the star too close
I think I pay attention until I try to write it down
and then I am never sure
to be sure is not what I aspire to
I want only what is mine
the parts that are lost in memory
the parts I swim toward again and again

HER STYLE

Early morning   sitting on her haunches
          in front of the bookcase
putting books and magazines in order
          her flannel nightgown a tent around her body

yesterday   lateafternoondespair
          toomany   chores   nomoney
for the bind she has got herself into
          not bindweed   that she could handle
          clip clip

               or maybe
let it grow up around her   hide her
          the lovely heart shaped leaves that go to red
               they would never find her
                              think her dead
          or runaway   that's her style   runaway

          from her tent wafts the warm odor of her body
she can't run away from that
                    like a weed she is boundtoit   lovesit
          this woman-rose   heart-flower   skin-musk

nothing works   she builds walls   hesitates
               waste   *waste*   *waste*   *all is waste*

          what is it she wants
the passion at the core of the music playing on her boombox
          some uncomplicated way to connect
               without drowning in someone else's pool

     there is no way out
                         do not resist
weed the beds   plant the bulbs   water
          think of it as your calling
                         what you were born for.

WAITING FOR SUNRISE

Since early morning I've been standing in the marsh,
a small sound and then two red-winged
blackbirds murmuring through the rushes.

There are bodies in here, sleek sides of fur
on tall animals who slip through narrow passages,
under low branches where I can't follow.

True dreams are like that, lose their way in the oozing
tracks of many deer floating over pussy willows.
I come upon a nest of wheat colored grasses

pressed down by resting bodies so recently unfolded
and fled without hurry I feel their heat, long for their community.
Since early morning I've been standing alone in the marsh.

Behind me, the house still in darkness; inside,
many dreams away, the woman who brought me here,
before us the already planned day.

I watch, wanting from the marsh some new thing. Or the heron.
Or a fox. Wanting the dawn to splendor the drifting, spring-
scented gray. Wanting the dreams I can't remember

and a certain lightness. This solid body I live in and call mine:
so much like the marsh, so much that is dark and wet and hidden.
Like the ducks on the far pond exploding into air.

Seeing them, want flowers like sedge, returns an old dream
about the absence of malice, the danger of need.
Since early morning I've been standing in this marsh.

EVERYTHING WAITING

The dark for light
empty road for cars
trees for warmth and leaves
the empty school for students
the house for lights
the kitchen for warm toast
and coffee smells
day for work
body for clothes
food and talk and touch
the feet for shoes and someplace to walk to
the ears for whatever sound and its own name
oh how the ears wait
or is it the heart
ears connect directly to the heart
so it is the heart that waits
this ♥ or the fist sized
fist shaped muscle in the chest
that waits just off center
waits and beats and waits and beats
while the body holding it waits
for the blood to make its rounds
waits out the twinges and pains
wakes in the night to them
wakes and wonders is it my heart
waits for morning and sunrise
and bodyrise a new day
and work and food and books
finally forgetting to wait because
everything she's ever wanted seems
there in those daylight hours
in those upstairs rooms
waiting just for her.

KAREN HERSETH WEE

ADOLESCENCE

I was eighteen on our last trip as a family
One day at the beach in San Diego
with a boy-cousin I hadn't known
Shy in my gangly body covered
with a black swimsuit
I lay with him on my tummy on the beach
dug my elbows into the sand for warmth
It was cloudy
We talked
Nothing much stands out—
certainly not what we said
Only the cloudy shade covering the beach
The pull of the distant waves on my prairie-flat body
My search for warmth as we remained out of water
My wanting him to like me
The gulls screaming and dipping down
toward the small pink shells
The burn I got
the backs of both thighs so red
so soon open sores   raw
I carried a vaselined pad in the car
for the next thousand miles
But my cousin cannot remember
us there at all
Lately I asked him
I can't remember anyone else on the beach that day
Not the suits they wore   nor their tans
nor the white skin oozing at the edges of cloth
nor their eyes behind fancy dark glasses
Someone must have been there   seen me
but only the gulls' cries stand out—
the wild punctuation
in the lost sentences we spoke

CYCLIST

You look beautiful in the morning . . .
the cyclist's voice, low-slung across the road

wrapped itself around me, cold, dressed in my
copper velvet robe, in the summer's early climbing sun

I looked east, but the sun blanked out his face
Only the blurry outline of a bearded man pressed upon me

that he might have meant what he had said
Still, he probably is the kind of man who raptures

flute-playing women are extremely sensuous, but is
too intent on his desperate quest to stop cycling

ANNIVERSARY, 1993

Somewhere on a trail
he is running
I wait
in a perfume
of white lilacs
on this listless swing

Somewhere in Minnesota
my daughter is crying
I hear
her far off
beyond mountains
beyond sunrise

BIRTHDAY REMEMBRANCE

We hike together
your father
your love, and I
Climb for hours
to a high valley basin
Watch you kiss
beneath ancient pine
In the distance
a fall of water
and a windy
soughing
refrain

We lean a minute
for steadiness
into this mountain
Eat humus and oranges
on a scree of rock
Pungent orange
oils the pads of our fingers
tinges everything
My eyes follow the spine
of Martin Ridge
A marmot whistles
You two decide
to stake no claim
on the other
for now

Far beneath us
the valley meanders
east, then west
harboring debris
from the heart's deep mine
We wonder aloud
at the human hunger

that can carve into stone
haul ore
from Earth's belly
leave a gaping hollowness
behind
Our own bones
lighten
in the moment
We lean
on our walking staffs
and descend

Later in lapidary
we grind chosen
stones into cabochons
leave them as gifts
in the hand of the other
moss agate, amethyst
rainbow obsidian—
hard beauty
formed in fire
and loss
eons ago

MOTHER'S DAY 1995

In the family photo taken in 1951
all our faces are unlined
pure beyond imagining
hers too—what was ahead was still ahead
the political life of many losses, some victories
the intimate life that eluded her
our trip to Ireland in 1965
my impatient rudeness to her thirty years later
as I shoveled gravel in the yard
of the new white clapboard house
on the Missouri just weeks
before her death

We two little girls in our cowgirl hats
and western shirts with fringe in the photograph
move toward adolescence with nonchalance
although Connie leans her weight a little bit
into Mom's akimbo arm
and our five-year-old brother
his pants pockets shaped
like holsters, stares with clear eyes
into the distance as if he already knows
about future fierce things

Two of the three of us fold
our hands, maybe mother does too
although today, staring
at this picture, I cannot tell
She always held them carefully in photographs
so that her ruined fingers, caught
and pulled away from her
when she was one year old
while hay binding with her brothers
wouldn't show Her thumb rests lightly
on Lars' little arm—she loved that son
Us too I know, but there was

something different in her love for him
And in the morning that she left us all
they were together, the two
of them alone, in an upper room at the farm

In the photo I am thin   the hips
that were to come and cradle
my own three within my womb
are still unformed
In all our gazes no hint
of the parenthood yet to come
that shows in hers

Mom wears a little hat
a fifties choker
necklace, earrings
and although the photograph
is black and white
I know the color of her dress
—rust brown—it is long and slim
long-sleeved, and when she stands
at her knees it flounces out
The color of the shirts we
children wear I can't recall
I do not lean
my hands hang
lightly at my sides
but notice, my eleven-
year-old lips are tense
What lies ahead is still ahead

MAKING IT—ONE WORD AT A TIME

Runes

My
words
trail
down
the
page
single
file
like
the
small
line
of
lost
stones
deep
in
a
forest
meadow
placed
there
years
ago
for
disre-
membered
purpose
by
un-
known
hands

After
all
the
words
meant
to
prevent

hurt
are
said
we've
arrived
at
a
place
where
we
can't
find
what
we've
come
for

Waking
The
Others

Gray
squirrels
skitter
coil
trails
up

and
down
the
great
Nor-
way
pine
by
the
cabin
window

One
day
is
all
we've
got
Our
need
to
talk
fades
in
the
presence
of
our
daugh-
ter
whose
needs
are
more
ap-
parent

to
us
than
our
own

Still
that
too
be-
comes
less
clear
when
in
the
late
after-
noon
high
clouds
lower
and
a
change
of
climate
sweeps
in
over
our
heads
We're
caught
in
the
middle—
sweaters
tied
around

our
hips
The
lake
a
mirror—
distant
memory
rip-
pling
our
di-
lemma
toward
us

Under
the
dock
the
foot
of
a
clam
inches
forward
across
a
sandy
pattern
of
waves
A
small
slant
of
sun
gets
through
To-

morrow
the
freezing

I
lie
awake
next
morning
for
hours
before
waking
the
others
The
response
I
don't
have
a
choice
do
I
dragging
like
the
clam
a
whole
history
of
debris

The
Walk
On
the
very

last
fall
day
with
summer
in
it
three
of
us
hike
deep
into
the
North-
woods
on
a
trail
faintly
re-
called
from
child-
hood

We
climb
and
des-
cend
into
some
of
the
earth's
great
hidden
bowls
hunting

for
The
Big
Meadow
and
The
CR
Carlson
Farm
We
do
not
find
them

Mean
clouds
come
in
Tower-
ing
roiling
masses
spitting
rain
ice
even

Every
conver-
sation
we
have
avoided
these
days
flares
in
the

sumac
flames
at
the
edges
of
our
eyes

Stalks
with
hitch-
hiker
seeds
grab
at
us
Finally
we
reach
a
two-
rut
road
Our
sense
of
danger
calms
Sense
of
direc-
tion
returns

I OFFER UP WILDFLOWERS

-a Litany of Names, Like Prayers in Prairie Smoke
for my Lost Mom

Spiderwort white   Yarrow   Wild Calla Lily
Wild Rose   &   purple Chives
Prairie Beard-Tongue licks the showy Yellow Lady Slipper
in the Morning's Glory
Prairie Smoke wafts over wild Columbine

Yellow Clover   purple and white in the fields
Wild Mustard   Marsh Marigold   a wonderful
bunch where the cold springs empty into Kabekona Lake
Globe Flower everywhere in ditches   all the way home
leaves like the Wild Geranium

Phlox at the ranch
Small Yellow flowers among the rushes on Sand Lake
In the water, single blooms
Horsetail (Snakeweed) its orangeish cone top
Showy Milkweed   Yellow Milkweed (Goatsbeard)

Milkweed—so soon to blossom
But Fleabane   Fleabane in the Pearly Everlasting
and the Howell's Everlasting   she called pussy toes

CONTRIBUTORS

NORTHFIELD WOMEN POETS began in the late 1960s, founded by Riki Kölbl Nelson and Karen Herseth Wee. Current membership is made up of women from Northfield and the surrounding area. The group meets weekly in member homes September through May, with monthly meetings during the summer. In 1993–94, the group published a chapbook series, one book by each member. *Tremors Vibrations Enough to Change the World* is the group's third anthology.

MARY MOORE EASTER poet/writer, dancer/choreographer, and a videomaker, is professor of dance at Carleton College, where, for seven years she was also director of African/African American Studies. In addition to a wide-ranging dance career, she is author of a poetry chapbook, *Walking from Origins*, published by Heywood Press in 1993. Her poems and essays have appeared in several magazines and anthologies including *The Hungry Mind Review* where she is a contributing editor. Her broadcast work includes creation of the radio show "To the Ancestor Spirits," and the video pieces "Some People" and "Mah."

ANDREA EEN is a violinist, violist and Hardanger fiddler who has performed solo and chamber recitals in Norway, France, Puerto Rico and Costa Rica. With the Plymouth Music series she has recorded numerous award-winning compact discs. She is a member of the first violin section of the Minnesota Opera Orchestra and an Associate Professor of Music at St. Olaf College. Returning to rural southern Minnesota in 1977 after an absence of ten years, Een began writing poetry as a deeply-felt response to the beauty of the landscape. In 1994 she published her first poetry chapbook, *Some Days We Name It Love*.

JIL EVANS, a full-time artist, has been interested in abstraction since beginning to paint sixteen years ago. She is still excited about its potential to evoke and elicit an experience of presence, however fleeting. Recently she began making abstract paintings based on observation of the natural world, and is finding that the spaces and qualities of light that she searched for in a painting such as "Padua" exist in overwhelming abundance around her. Of poetry she says, "I need poetry, and the poet's observations of nature and how it acts to help shape us. Poetry breaks down my rigidity in thinking and seeing. How one 'gets-at' content in painting seems very similiar to the act of poetry, for the connections are made intuitively through experiencing a work that embodies leaps in understanding in its very form, rather than explaining them."

MARIE VOGL GERY says, "To be a poet one must exhume the exact word from the normal detritus that fills one's vocabulary. For me, a poet is a digger in the garden of words and weeds. In order for me to create a poem, I need to dig far beyond the usual. Sometimes I write an essay but line it out as a poem. When I sing in the kitchen I rhyme: songs that go no farther than the sink. I write because if I did not write I would disappear—and finally after all the rest is gone, the letters and poems of the dead are what we all remember. I tell stories, write poems, plant and weed gardens, watch birds, love my husband and children, and value my friends.

SUSAN THURSTON HAMERSKI was born in Mankato, Minnesota, and grew up on a farm just north of Lake Crystal on land that didn't seem certain about being prairie. She earned her bachelor of arts degree from Mankato State University, where one of her favorite teachers had gone, and a master of arts degree from Hamline, where one of her favorite writers taught. She has worked as a journalist, shopkeeper, college administrator and teacher. She and her husband Michael have almost completed restoration of a 1904 home, which they share with their dog Molly. Susan is finishing a novel entitled *Ciphers*.

SIGI LEONHARD, born in Germany, pursued her education there, in France and at Stanford University where she received her PhD in 1982. She teaches German language and literature, with an emphasis on women's writing at Carleton college, writes and publishes scholarly articles, poetry and fiction, and takes care of two-year-old Nadja, her daughter and muse. She lives in St. Paul with her partner Alan, Nadja, Buster the cat, a bunch of raccoons and numerous ghosts of the past, present and future.

JOANNE MAKELA has written poetry since second grade. She won a grant from the Loft for performing poetry in 1992 and from Forecast Public Art Affairs in 1994. She believes in finding public forums for the written word and in returning the voice of the poet to its rightful place as a chronicler of the times. Makela runs a thrift shop in Northfield and helps raise her three children, Alex, Zach and Elizabeth. She enjoys performing music and poetry with her multi-generational, all-woman group, *Shopping Nirvana*.

RIKI KÖLBL NELSON, artist and writer, has exhibited her work and given readings here and abroad. She has worked as artist in residence in schools and elderhostels, taught at St. Olaf College and the University of Minnesota. She holds an MA in English from the University of North Carolina, Chapel Hill and an MFA in studio art from the University of Minnesota. Her publications include a bi-lingual collection of poems, *Borders/Grenzen*, and a chapbook, *The Fall Heart*. She lives with her spouse Eric in Northfield, attends son Benno's rock-concerts in Minneapolis, sometimes gives performances as Roosterwoman, and sings, struts, crows.

MARCELLA TAYLOR grew up in the Bahamas and is of African, Seminole and Scottish descent. Her poems have appreared in forty journals and anthologies, in a collection, *The Lost Daughter*, and in a chapbook, *Songs for the Arawak*. She was a Loft Mentor winner and has been awarded six residencies including The Helene Wurlitzer Foundation in Taos and The Camargo Foundation in Cassis, France. She teaches at St. Olaf College.

BEVERLY VOLDSETH, despairing of ever holding down a real job for longer than three years, takes solace in Louis Simpson's words: "You were born to waste your life. / You were born to this middleclass life. / As others before you / were born to walk in procession to the temple, singing." Editor and publisher of Black Hat Press, she publishes *Rag Mag*, a semi-annual lit mag, and has several books of poems, one book of prose and one tape by midwest (and one French) writers on her booklist. For inspiration she spends time with her three daughters and five grandchildren and visits Mille Lacs where she can never get enough of lake, sky, loons, trees, flowers, air, stones.

KAREN HERSETH WEE, South Dakota cowgirl, artist, mother of artists, and transplant to academia, is a founding member of Northfield Women Poets. She has two books of poems (for which she also did cover designs and layout) published by Black Hat Press: *The Book of Hearts*, a 1993 Book Award nominee, (first printing sold out), and *Baksheesh, journal and poems*, 1994. Her work is included in NWP's 1984 anthology *Absorb the Colors* and *A Rich Salt Place*, 1986. Her chapbook is *Before Language*. She is a 1995 recipient of a two-week residency at Norcroft, a writing retreat for women on the North Shore of Lake Superior.